NEW ZEALAND *a photo tour*

PHOTOGRAPHY BY BOB McCREE • TEXT BY BRIAN O'FLAHERTY

REED

reed publishing (NZ) Ltd
Te Karuhi tā tāpui o Reed (Aotearoa)

Established in 1907, Reed is New Zealand's largest
book publisher, with over 300 titles in print.

For details on all these books visit our website:
www.reed.co.nz

Published by Reed Books, a division of Reed Publishing (NZ) Ltd, 39 Rawene Rd, Birkenhead, Auckland.
Associated companies, branches and representatives throughout the world.

© Reed Publishing (NZ) Ltd 2003
Photos © Bob McCree 2003

TEXT Brian O'Flaherty/Punaromia
DESIGN Julie McDermid/Punaromia
COVER DESIGN Jacinda Torrance, Verso Visual Communications

FRONT Medlands Beach, Great Barrier Island, Hauraki Gulf.
REAR Mountains in Tongariro National Park, central North Island. Mt Ngauruhoe (*on right*) behind Mt
Pukekaikiore, with Mt Tongariro beyond at left.
TITLE PAGE Autumn at Lake Wanaka, Otago.

ISBN 0 7900 0923 4

Printed in China

CONTENTS

Introduction 4

Northland and Auckland 6

Coromandel, Waikato and Bay of Plenty 14

East Coast, Volcanic Plateau and Taranaki 22

Hawke's Bay, Wairarapa and Wellington 30

Nelson and Marlborough 38

Kaikoura and Canterbury 46

West Coast, Otago and Fiordland 54

INTRODUCTION

New Zealand is blessed with a great stock of scenic attractions. The country is a world in miniature, with everything from active volcanoes and geysers to lakes, rivers and majestic snow-capped mountains.

New Zealand: A Photo Tour provides a brief journey around the dramatically different landscapes of the country's varied regions, towns and cities, from the subtropical north to the magnificent wilderness of Fiordland in the south.

Geologically, New Zealand is a relatively new land, arising on the edge of the supercontinent of Gondwanaland between 600 and 300 million years ago, then breaking away and, by the process of seafloor spreading, set adrift into the Pacific Ocean. The journey halted some 60 million years ago, leaving New Zealand as a lonely group of islands, one of the most isolated landmasses of its size in the world.

The processes that formed the country continue to shape it today. New Zealand sits astride two tectonic plates, the Australian and Pacific, and their collision pushes up the North Island's ranges and the Southern Alps. Snow from the Alps feeds rivers and numerous glaciers, which in the past have gouged out deep valleys now filled with lakes or fiords. Plate collision also provides fire to the central North Island volcanoes and heat for geysers and hot springs.

In human terms, New Zealand is also young, being one of the last lands to be peopled, with Maori arriving in Aotearoa from eastern Polynesia around one thousand years ago. The first settlers made sense of their new land with a mythology that depicted natural features as the sites of deeds of gods, demons or ancestors. Maori found an untouched environment with flora and fauna that had developed for millions of years in isolation from the rest of the world. Their new country teemed with countless birds, including flightless species like the giant moa, with the only land-based mammals being small bats.

Dutch explorer Abel Tasman visited in 1642, and christened the land Nieuw Zeeland, after the Netherlands province of Zeeland. English navigator James Cook in 1769 was another early visitor, mapping and naming natural features, and experiencing some of the first eventful meetings of two peoples. The first Europeans were usually temporary visitors lured by the country's natural riches of

whales, seals and timber. Later, immigrants from the British Isles arrived to build towns and clear the forest for farms. They changed the face of the country forever, and despite a Treaty guaranteeing Maori possession of their lands, fisheries and resources, the thirst for land led to wars that alienated land from Maori and changed their culture irrevocably.

Today New Zealand is a vibrant young nation. The population of four million has a bicultural base, Maori and European, and is becoming increasingly multicultural, and the country is forging its own unique character, culture and identity.

NORTHLAND AND AUCKLAND

Basking in a warm, subtropical climate, Northland has become the 'Winterless North' to its residents, who also enjoy the quiet isolation of its small towns and settlements. This northern tip of New Zealand is also known for its forests of kauri trees, survivors of the ancient wilderness. The region's key attraction, however, is a beautiful and varied coastline of innumerable island-studded bays, mangrove-lined harbours and endless stretches of sandy beach.

Northland's twin coasts are starkly different. The exposed western coast has long, surf-pounded beaches, some doubling as national highways, with dunes reaching far inland. At the tip of the country, just beyond Cape Reinga, the Tasman Sea and Pacific Ocean meet in a dramatic swirl of currents. The sheltered and indented east coast features bays and harbours, rocky shores and sandy beaches, along which the pohutukawa can be seen, clothed in crimson flowers in summer, making it New Zealand's Christmas tree.

The North's great drawcard is the Bay of Islands, with its numerous sheltered inlets and islands. In summer holidaymakers are lured by the beaches and myriad activities including water sports, sailing, and dolphin and whale watching cruises. Visitors are also drawn year-round by the region's historical sites, as Northland and Auckland were among the first parts of the country to be settled. The warm climate, abundant marine life, forests and sheltered harbours appealed to Maori, and also attracted early European settlers.

In the bay, the characterful Russell, formerly Kororareka, was established around 1800, and was New Zealand's first permanent European settlement and its first capital. Across the water, the reserve at Waitangi is where Maori and Pakeha signed a founding treaty.

The Auckland region encompasses four cities in a sprawl rivalling Los Angeles, but also boasts over 48 volcanoes, 50 islands, 22 regional parks and three marine reserves, as well as many beaches. In the northeast, the Waitemata Harbour opens to the sheltered Hauraki Gulf, with its diverse islands and islets, some populated, others sanctuaries for endangered wildlife. In the southwest is the Manukau Harbour, opening to the Tasman Sea, which lashes rocky headlands of the forest-clad Waitakere Ranges. As the 'City of Sails', Auckland's waterways are always alive with craft of all descriptions.

Auckland is the country's commercial heart and its most cosmopolitan and multicultural region, with a wide range of influences adding to its vibrancy. Along with the majority of the country's Maori, it has the world's largest population of Pacific Islanders, as well as many newer immigrants from Asia. Although a large city, it is easy to escape to the outdoors, for a stroll along city beaches on the scenic waterfront, or to enjoy the views from volcano summits.

PREVIOUS PAGES: The Tasman Sea and Pacific Ocean meet in a swirl of currents at the tip of Northland (*page 4*). Maori motifs (*page 5*). The Whare Runanga (meeting house) at Waitangi in the Bay of Islands, Northland, with its beautifully decorated interior, was built in 1940 to mark the centenary of the signing of the Treaty of Waitangi (*page 6*). Holidaymakers enjoy the surf, sand and sun at Mathesons Bay, Northland (*page 7*).

ABOVE LEFT: The lighthouse at Cape Reinga.

ABOVE RIGHT: Waiotemarama Falls, south of Hokianga Harbour on Northland's west coast. Plants luxuriate in the region's subtropical climate.

OPPOSITE: Hokianga Harbour's north head comprises giant sand dunes, driven and piled up by the westerly winds.

OPPOSITE: Auckland city's commercial centre spills down to the Waitemata Harbour, always busy with shipping and pleasure craft.

ABOVE: Aucklanders have easy access to the outdoors, with city beaches like Howick popular with swimmers and windsurfers, boaties and yachties. Annual regattas fill the harbour with yachts of all sizes.

ABOVE: At Muriwai Beach on Auckland's west coast, a colony of Australasian gannets can be viewed from July to October on their nests atop a rock stack and mainland cliffs. Young birds spend two to four years in Australian waters before returning to New Zealand to breed.

ABOVE: Once a base for fishing fleets, the Viaduct Basin on Auckland's waterfront was revitalised for New Zealand's defence of the America's Cup, yachting's greatest prize, in 2000 and 2003. Cafés, restaurants and apartment buildings were built around super-yacht berths and the bases of challenging syndicates.

CENTRE: Westhaven is one of several marinas around Auckland's shoreline. The city boasts one of the highest rates of boat ownership in the world as well as many world-class sailors.

FAR RIGHT: The Sky City Casino's landmark Sky Tower brightens the night sky. At 328 metres, the Tower is New Zealand's tallest structure, and includes an observation platform and revolving restaurant.

COROMANDEL, WAIKATO AND BAY OF PLENTY

At the feet of Coromandel's rugged mountain spine lie some of the country's finest beaches and most beautiful coastal scenery. South of Auckland, the Coromandel Peninsula separates the Hauraki Gulf from the Bay of Plenty; its intricate indented coastline is a spectacular seascape of harbours, bays, beaches and islands. From November to January, the coast is ablaze with pohutukawa trees in bloom.

The densely forested interior was the scene of early enterprises in the 19th century: felling kauri trees, digging fossilised kauri resin from the ground, and extracting gold from crushed quartz. Today, small towns on the Coromandel are a haven for craftspeople and artists.

From Thames, the scenic Pacific Coast Highway skirts the stony beaches and rocky headlands of the Firth of Thames on its way north to Coromandel Harbour, then on through bays to Colville, and around the tip of the peninsula. On the east coast, sheltered by the ranges, lie more beaches and blue sea, harbours, bays and offshore islands. Popular resorts abound in this holiday mecca, such as at Whitianga, Whangapoua, Hahei, Tairua and Pauanui. At Hot Water Beach, hot springs seep through the sand, and visitors can scoop their own hot pools at the edge of the sea.

Spreading out across the plains south of the Coromandel, the Waikato is a region of rich pastureland, famed for its dairy production and thoroughbred studs. Its name is taken from the river

that runs through it, whose full name is Waikato-taniwha-rau, the flowing water of a hundred taniwha - the monsters that lurk in its pools. New Zealand's longest river, the Waikato travels some 425 kilometres from Lake Taupo to the Tasman Sea. Along the way it whirls through nine hydro-electric powerhouses before meandering across the plains and through Hamilton, the hub of the region's farming industry, renowned for its riverside gardens.

Southeast of Coromandel sweeps the Bay of Plenty, encompassing several offshore islands, including the active volcano of White Island, popular beaches, and harbours and estuaries. Explorer James Cook sailed into the bay in October 1769, naming it for the thriving settlements of Maori who greeted him in friendly fashion.

The resort of Mt Maunganui sits on the seaward side of Tauranga Harbour, the region's busiest port servicing the city that is the centre of a flourishing dairying and fruit-growing district, known as the 'kiwifruit capital of the world'. The warmth and sunshine also attract holidaymakers and retirees.

Inland Bay of Plenty is best known for the city of Rotorua, one of New Zealand's premier tourist destinations, world famous for its plentiful geysers, hot springs and bubbling mudpools, spas, numerous lakes, trout fishing, bush walks and farm shows. It is also home to a large Maori population, whose distinctive cultural activities are a major drawcard.

PREVIOUS PAGES: The resort town of Mount Maunganui viewed from atop the 223-metre extinct dome volcano of Mauao. The town separates the well-known Main Beach, a popular surfing and swimming site, from Tauranga Harbour (*page 14*).

    The Coromandel was the scene of gold rushes in the 1860s. The Assay House in Coromandel township is one of the many relics of the era (*page 15*).

FAR LEFT: The sun-soaked Coromandel Peninsula has a rugged bush-clad interior and a coastline fringed with pristine white sand beaches and quiet bays, and small estuaries like Whangapoua.

CENTRE: The clear water of Medlands Beach on rugged and scenic Great Barrier Island, the largest island in the Hauraki Gulf.

ABOVE: Visitors to isolated Fletcher Bay, at the very tip of the Coromandel Peninsula, enjoy deserted beaches and forest and coastal walks.

FAR LEFT: Set alongside the Waikato River, the popular Hamilton Gardens presents 100 different garden themes from around the world, including Chinese styles from various dynasties.

LEFT: The *Waipa Delta* plies the Waikato River as it flows past Hamilton's parks and gardens.

BELOW: Manu Bay, at Raglan on the Waikato's west coast, draws surfers from around the world to its often superb waves and its renowned long left-hand break. The town of Raglan is a laid-back seaside getaway, with a sheltered harbour ideal for windsurfing, swimming and boating.

FAR LEFT: One of the many colourful hot-air balloons from all over the world that take to the skies for the annual Balloons over Waikato festival.

CENTRE: Steam rises from thermal springs around the Maori village of Ohinemutu on the edge of Lake Rotorua. The Anglican church of St Faiths here features an interior decorated with Maori carvings and panel work, as well as a stained-glass window of Christ seemingly walking on the waters of the lake beyond.

ABOVE: Inland Bay of Plenty's lakes and rivers are popular with anglers and outdoor adventurers, such as these whitewater rafters below Okere Falls, the outlet of Lake Rotorua.

EAST COAST, VOLCANIC PLATEAU AND TARANAKI

Isolated, sparsely populated and beautiful, the East Coast has its own leisurely pace and relaxed atmosphere. Around half of the population are Maori, and their small villages and marae are landmarks along the coast. From Opotiki eastwards, the East Cape forms a roughly triangular promontory of steep hills above rocky shores or long beaches broken by headlands. The highest peak on the cape, Mt Hikurangi, is the first place in New Zealand to see the new dawn. The mountain is sacred to Maori, who believe it was the first part of the fish hauled from the sea by the demi-god Maui – the fish that became the North Island.

North of Opotiki are driftwood-laden coves and peaceful bays such as Te Kaha, Whanarua Bay and Waihau Bay. Once around East Cape, the eastern coast unfurls in its many quiet, golden sand beaches, such as at Tokomaru Bay, Anaura Bay and Tolaga Bay.

At Gisborne, the river flats spreading out behind the city provide the conditions for orchards and vineyards to flourish, with the warm, dry climate ideal for growing grapes. It was near Gisborne on 9 October 1769 that Captain James Cook and crew from the *Endeavour* went ashore, the first Europeans to set foot in New Zealand. Their encounter with the locals ended badly, however, with a misunderstanding resulting in several Maori being killed.

In the centre of the North Island, the Volcanic Plateau incorporates Taupo, the country's largest

lake, sitting in the caldera formed by some of the most violent eruptions ever to occur on earth. Below this region, the Pacific tectonic plate slides beneath the Australian, resulting in a range of volcanic activity, most evident in the spectacular peaks of Tongariro National Park, an area of outstanding natural beauty offering excellent trout fishing, snow sports and adventure excursions on rivers, lakes and mountains. Tongariro, Ngauruhoe and Ruapehu are the three active volcanoes that dominate the landscape of the national park, which became only the second such park in the world after the mountains were gifted to the nation by Ngati Tuwharetoa chief Te Heuheu in 1894. To Maori, the mountains have traditionally been the domain of Ruamoko, the god of earthquake and volcanic fire. Ruamoko vented his wrath most recently in 1995–96, when Ruapehu erupted spectacularly.

Plate collision is also responsible for Mt Taranaki/Egmont in the west of the North Island, surrounded by its fertile ring plain that supports a thriving dairy industry as well as numerous parks and gardens. In Maori myth, Taranaki once lived with the other mountains in the centre of the island. They were all male except the lovely Pihanga, for whose attention they battled, hurling fire at each other. Tongariro was the victor and the defeated mountains had to leave. Taranaki was banished 150 kilometres to the west, where it now forms a stunning backdrop to the city of New Plymouth.

PREVIOUS PAGES: The country's longest wharf extends 660 metres into Tolaga Bay. It served for 40 years from 1929, seeing meat and wool shipped from the region's farms (*page 22*). The dramatic cone of Mt Ngauruhoe rises 2290 metres on the Volcanic Plateau (*page 23*).

ABOVE: Beneath the Volcanic Plateau, superheated groundwater circulates through the upper layers of the crust, and in places breaks through the surface. At Craters of the Moon, near Taupo, visitors admire the many vigorous hot springs, steam vents and mudpools.

RIGHT: Mt Ruapehu, at 2797 metres the largest mountain in the Tongariro National Park, is home to both of the North Island's skifields, Whakapapa (*pictured*) and Turoa.

LEFT: An angler prepares for fly fishing at the mouth of the Waitahanui River, which flows into Lake Taupo. New Zealand's largest lake and the rivers flowing into it offer some of the country's best fishing for brown and rainbow trout.

ABOVE: Majestic volcanoes dominate Tongariro National Park. The youngest is the stratovolcano of Ngauruhoe (*on right*) rising behind the low cone of Pukekaikiore, with the peak of Tongariro beyond at left. Ngauruhoe began life as a new vent on the eroded southern flanks of Mt Tongariro and still occasionally erupts ash and lava in fiery displays.

ABOVE: Golf course at Kinloch, on the western side of Lake Taupo. The region's attractions include international golf links, trout fishing, thermal areas, and the hiking trails and skifields of Tongariro National Park.

RIGHT: The isolated volcanic cone of Mt Taranaki/Egmont, 2518 metres high, dominates the western North Island and towers over the city of New Plymouth, centre of the area's dairying and energy industries and known for its parks, gardens and rhododendron festivals.

HAWKE'S BAY, WAIRARAPA AND WELLINGTON

The Hawke's Bay and Wairarapa regions encompass fertile farmland lying in the lee of the central mountain ranges. Hawke's Bay takes its name from a large scallop-shaped bay of surf-washed beaches with the city of Napier at its centre and, at its southern limit, the eroded peaks of Cape Kidnappers, home to a mainland colony of Australasian gannets. These are the last peaceful beaches before the dramatic, but often inhospitable, cliff-lined coast of the Wairarapa begins, stretching between two capes named by Captain Cook – Turnagain and Palliser.

Hawke's Bay hill country sheep stations give way to fertile plains nearer the coast, traditionally used for growing fruit and vegetables but more recently also for wine production, as growers take advantage of the hot, dry summers and stony soils. The plentiful sunshine and a fine coastal position only add to Napier's attractiveness. Around the city are popular swimming and surfing beaches, and its Marine Parade is a beautiful seaside boulevard. Napier and its twin city of Hastings were all but destroyed in a catastrophic earthquake in 1931. They were rebuilt in the Art Deco and Spanish Mission style architecture popular at the time, for which they are now renowned.

The Wairarapa is sheep country, with numerous farms on the plains east of the central ranges and on the hill country near the coast. The farms were

wrought from the bush largely by Danish and Norwegian settlers, whose Scandinavian legacy survives in the names of local towns and the surnames of their inhabitants.

The area's once sleepy towns have been rejuvenated as weekend retreats for city folk from over the Rimutaka Range in Wellington. Martinborough and Greytown have come alive with cafés and restaurants since finding themselves at the centre of a small wine region with a big reputation.

Wellington, the capital city, sits in the steep hills that surround a beautiful harbour on the southwestern tip of the North Island – and right on top of a fault line, resulting in the ever-present threat of earthquakes. Pressure from below is matched by gales above, as 'Windy Wellington' is exposed to strong winds from Cook Strait, across which ferries ply to the South Island. When rain and wind abate, though, Wellington is perfectly picturesque. Since 1865 the seat of government, Wellington is a cosmopolitan city with a character all its own, its hills studded with Victorian wooden houses, contrasting with the high-rises of the central commercial district, which opens onto a bustling refurbished waterfront, filled with cafés, restaurants and bars. The city markets itself as a centre of culture and the arts, with the biennial International Festival of the Arts and the national museum, Te Papa Tongarewa, major drawcards.

PREVIOUS PAGES: A cable car has carried passengers to Wellington's hillside suburb of Kelburn and the city's university since 1902 (*page 30*). Wines maturing in oak barrels in the cellars of the Church Road winery in Taradale, Hawke's Bay, which incorporates the former McDonald winery (*page 31*).

LEFT: Fountains, statues and gardens are part of Napier's Marine Parade, lined with stately Norfolk Island pines.

ABOVE: Napier's Masonic Hotel is among many examples of the streamlined Art Deco architectural style with its bold plaster motifs.

RIGHT: White Bay Lavender Farm sits on the small fertile plain of the Esk Valley, carved out by the Esk River, in the lee of sunburnt hills north of Napier.

LEFT: Over 150 years after planting the first vineyards in Hawke's Bay, Mission Vineyards is still producing wines. Founded and still managed by the Catholic Society of Mary, the Mission incorporates a winery and restored former seminary buildings.

ABOVE: Castlepoint is one of the few resorts on the windswept Wairarapa coast. The automated lighthouse, built in 1913, sends its beam far out into the Pacific, guiding shipping into Cook Strait and Wellington.

ABOVE: Pride of place on Wellington's redeveloped harbourfront is the national museum, Te Papa Tongarewa. Opened in 1989, Te Papa offers many interactive displays as well as more traditional galleries.

RIGHT: Seen from the waterfront, houses cling to the steep hillsides around Wellington's beautiful deep-water harbour.

FAR RIGHT: On fine days, when freezing gales aren't blowing in from Cook Strait, the 'Windy City' of Wellington is a magical place. On calm, clear nights the city is a sea of lights from harbour to hillsides.

NELSON AND MARLBOROUGH

Nelson and Marlborough encompass the top of the South Island, an area of stunning natural beauty that draws visitors to its snow-capped mountains, forests, lakes, rivers and beaches. At its far northwestern corner is Farewell Spit, a curved finger of sand that is an internationally recognised habitat for shore birds.

Much of this natural heritage is preserved in Nelson's three national parks: Kahurangi, Nelson Lakes and Abel Tasman. The last is the country's smallest but best known, stretching along a serene coastline of bush-edged, golden-sand beaches in Tasman Bay, one of the most popular summer destinations for walkers and kayakers. The Abel Tasman Coastal Track that meanders around the coast is one of New Zealand's most attractive and accessible walks. The bay and the national park take their names from Dutch explorer Abel Tasman, the first European to reach New Zealand in 1642. In nearby Golden Bay he made contact with Maori, who, suspicious of the strange visitors, attacked and killed four of his crew.

The Marlborough Sounds were created by gradual sinking of the land beneath them and rising sea levels, resulting in numerous idyllic waterways that twist and turn beneath forested hills. The largest of these labyrinths is Queen Charlotte Sound, the passage for all shipping connecting Wellington to Picton at the head of the sound, including the interisland ferries.

Maori settled early in the Nelson region, drawn by the sunshine, fertile coastal lowland and access to the West Coast and places further south. These features proved attractive to some of the earliest European immigrants, too, who started to build a town in Nelson, on the seaside in Tasman Bay. With many fine buildings dating from the 1850s and 1860s, Nelson is now known as the hub of the local fruit-growing and forestry industries, as well as a thriving arts and crafts scene. Annual events include the Arts Festival, Taste Nelson festival, and the Wearable Art Awards, showcasing unusual and fantastical apparel.

Marlborough is synonymous with the sounds – and with sauvignon blanc. The maze of waterways in the sounds draws visitors in boats, yachts and kayaks. Local aquaculture produces some of the area's bounty, including prized oysters, mussels and salmon. The Wairau Plains reach inland, spreading out between the ranges. The plains around Blenheim were once swampland drained for pastoral farming then used for horticulture and, more recently, planted in endless rows of grapevines. The sun-baked soils put New Zealand on the world wine map in the mid-1980s with herbaceous sauvignon blancs, and now Marlborough is the country's largest wine-growing district, with an international reputation. Local winemakers and food producers show off their products in the popular annual Marlborough Wine and Food Festival.

PREVIOUS PAGES: Queen Charlotte Sound is the largest of the Marlborough Sounds and the sea passage for interisland shipping (*page 38*).
Broadgreen House in Nelson is a two-storey cob house built around 1855 and carefully furnished in the period (*page 39*).

ABOVE: The Wairau Plains are bordered by hill country, home to sheep and cattle farms, while the plains, mostly reclaimed from swamps, grow a variety of fruit crops as well as top wine-producing grapes.

RIGHT: Marlborough's wines captured the world's attention in the 1980s and it is now New Zealand's largest wine district with over 50 wineries and around 5000 hectares of bearing vines, including these ones in the well-known Rapaura Road area near Blenheim.

LEFT: Blenheim is the centre of Marlborough's wine district, and venue for the popular annual Food and Wine Festival. Seymour Square's clock tower is a memorial to those from the area who died in the two world wars.

ABOVE: Nelsonians are proud of their many fine historic buildings, such as the city's traditional symbol, the Art Deco cathedral, begun in 1925 and finally consecrated in 1972.

FAR RIGHT: The easily accessible Kaiteriteri in Nelson is one of the South Island's most popular family beach resorts.

44

FAR LEFT: The Abel Tasman National Park stretches along a stunning coastline of sandy, bush-edged beaches, such as Tinline Bay. The coast features one of New Zealand's Great Walks and is also a popular sea kayaking venue.

CENTRE: The three-day trek along the coastal track in Abel Tasman National Park is one of the country's most popular summer walks. Visitors can be picked up or dropped off at any point on the coast by water taxi. Here walkers depart from the golden crescent of Totaranui Beach at the western end of the coastal track.

ABOVE: On the northwestern tip of the South Island, Farewell Spit extends a 26 kilometre-long finger of sand dunes, shell banks and marshland. The conservation area here is regarded as an internationally important wetland and bird sanctuary, alive in summer with thousands of migrant wading birds from the Arctic tundra.

KAIKOURA AND CANTERBURY

South of Marlborough, the Kaikoura region lies in a spectacular setting, its rocky coastline backed by the steeply rising foothills of the Seaward Kaikoura mountains, which in winter carry a mantle of snow. The small town of Kaikoura, set in its own beautiful bay, has traditionally been a fishing port renowned for its rock lobster, or crayfish, but in recent years activities such as whale watching and swimming with dolphins and seals have put it on the tourist map. Out from the Kaikoura coast the seafloor drops steeply to form part of a huge deep-water canyon that runs from Antarctica past Kaikoura and into the Pacific Ocean. Along with other marine mammals, sperm, humpback and southern right whales can be viewed close to the coastline as they migrate in these waters.

Once over the dry hill country of North Canterbury, the main highway south rolls down into the vast Canterbury Plains. In the east are the snow-covered mountains of the Southern Alps, whose retreating glaciers long ago gouged out troughs now filled by elongated lakes such as Tekapo and Pukaki. Across these plains early Maori hunted the large flightless moa, often setting fire to the lowland forest to drive them from cover. When Maori ventured into the mountains, they found passes leading to the West Coast, such as Arthur's Pass and Burkes Pass, routes that today's highways follow, and they encountered and named the country's highest peak, Aoraki/Mt Cook.

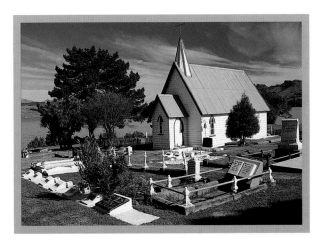

The great rivers that flow from the mountains to the Pacific deposited their silt and gravel to form the plains, and eventually linked the mainland with the island of present-day Banks Peninsula, formed by two volcanoes whose final violent eruptions blew out their crater walls, letting the sea in and creating two superb natural harbours, Lyttelton and Akaroa.

A shipload of French emigrants settled in Akaroa in 1840, and their influence is still evident today. This was an attempt to colonise the country, but the English had just beaten them to it by signing the Treaty of Waitangi. Ten years later Church of England settlers landed at Lyttelton and made their way over the hills to the plains. There they established the English Gothic town of Christchurch, today the South Island's largest city. Sheep farming soon became the region's mainstay as farms spread across the plains into the high country. Present-day Christchurch is a modern, orderly city, with a high quota of cafés, restaurants and bars, and enjoying easy access to the skifields and mountains of the Southern Alps. The city's 'Englishness' survives in the many tree-filled parks and gardens, a neo-Gothic cathedral dominating the square, numerous old stone buildings, and punts gliding on the tree-lined Avon River meandering through its centre. Popular sites include the Christchurch Arts Centre, a recently completed Art Gallery, the Antarctic Centre and the expansive Hagley Park.

PREVIOUS PAGES: The Avon meanders through Christchurch's leafy suburbs, such as at Mona Vale (*pictured*) and through Hagley Park and the city. At the old Antigua boatsheds you can begin a leisurely trip down the river on a canoe, paddle boat, row boat or punt (*page 46*).

The wooden church at Rapaki is one of many historic buildings around Lyttelton Harbour (*page 47*).

OPPOSITE: A sperm whale dives off Kaikoura. Marine mammal-watching tours allow visitors to see fur seals, orca, and minke, humpback, pilot and southern right whales.

ABOVE: Kaikoura is synonymous with crayfish or rock lobster, the region's delicacy, available from cafés, restaurants and roadside stalls.

RIGHT: Many of North Canterbury's hills have weathered into striking cliffs, like these ones at Gore Bay, known as the Cathedrals.

OPPOSITE: Christchurch's Cathedral Square has as its centre the Anglican Cathedral, consecrated in 1881, with its 63-metre spire. A new addition is the modern chalice sculpture by Neil Dawson.

ABOVE: Akaroa is a peaceful harbour on the south of Banks Peninsula. The town of Akaroa on the harbourside was established by French settlers in 1840 and today its streets and houses retain their French names and descendants of the original settlers still live in the area.

FAR LEFT: From Christchurch the Canterbury Plains sweep inland to the foothills of the Southern Alps, such as at Broken River. Sheep farming remains an essential part of the region's economy.

CENTRE: Lyttelton Harbour is connected to Christchurch by rail and road tunnels under the Port Hills. Boat cruises are the most popular way of exploring the harbour's many tranquil bays, such as Governor's Bay.

ABOVE: Castle Hill station is one of many sheep stations in the foothills and high country to the west of the Canterbury Plains. Many carry large flocks of fine-wool merino sheep.

WEST COAST, OTAGO AND FIORDLAND

Remote, pristine and spectacularly scenic, the West Coast runs 600 kilometres along the rugged Tasman Sea coastline, with wild, dramatic beaches, steep glaciers, swift snow-fed rivers, and bush-clad hills sweeping up to the peaks of the Southern Alps. It is a region of unspoiled beauty, incessant rain and lashing seas. However, it has not been the most welcoming environment for visitors. Maori trekked across the alpine passes to collect pounamu (nephrite jade or greenstone) for their tools, weapons and ornaments, but did not stay long. Neither did Europeans, until gold was discovered near the Taramakau River in 1864. Thousands flocked to sluice, pan and dredge, and frontier towns sprang up overnight. With the bulk of the gold and the hopeful miners gone, those who stayed turned to exploiting the region's coal and timber. Today, logging bans have safeguarded the remaining native forests and the indefatigable 'Coasters' have turned to tourism for income. It is untouched wilderness that enthralls visitors: the limestone wonders at Punakaiki, and the Franz Josef and Fox glaciers, are major attractions.

Gold lured people to Otago, too. Thousands of prospectors scoured the hills and rivers of Central Otago after gold was found in the Arrow River in 1862. Only a few of their settlements remain today, in a region of vast skies, dramatic schist outcrops, rolling expanses of burnt-gold tussock, alpine lakes, searingly hot summers and freezing winters.

Maori moa hunters once roamed the forested hills and settled along the Otago coast. They left as moa numbers declined and the climate cooled. The first European settlers arrived from Scotland in 1848, and when gold was discovered, the region's population of 12,000 quadrupled, and the coastal city of Dunedin boomed with the new wealth generated. Most of its architectural heritage remains intact and the cityscape includes grand Victorian and Edwardian neo-Gothic stone buildings. The historic University of Otago was the country's first, and today Dunedin's student population drives the local arts and entertainment scene.

The new gold in Otago is tourism. Visitors flock to the Queenstown area, with its mountains towering over glacier-scoured lakes, and numerous adventure activities, from jet-boating and white-water rafting to mountain biking and skiing.

Queenstown is a departure point for the southwest and the fiords, mountains, famous walks and unrivalled scenery of Fiordland National Park, the country's largest national park. From the rugged coastline 16 glacier-gouged sounds weave their way inland, the mountains on their sides plunging sheer into the dark water. After rain, the mountainsides roar with numerous waterfalls. In this remote, raw and powerful region, one of the world's greatest wilderness areas, water and mountains combine to create a dramatic and breathtaking landscape, a grand finale to the visitor's tour of New Zealand.

PREVIOUS PAGES: The Southern Alps loom over the West Coast's wild rocky beaches, seen here near Greymouth (*page 54*).

Kayakers explore the extensive lagoon and tidal flats at Okarito, the country's largest unmodified wetland (*page 55*).

LEFT: Paparoa National Park is noted for its coastal scenery. At Punakaiki columns of spray thunder through blowholes in the 'pancake' layers of stratified limestone.

BELOW: Franz Josef Glacier (*pictured*) along with the Fox Glacier, are the most easily accessible of over 60 glaciers in the Westland/Tai Poutini National Park.

ABOVE: Lake Matheson near Fox Glacier township in Westland National Park provides perfect reflections of the forest that fringes it, along with the breathtaking panorama of the Southern Alps. The lake fills a depression created thousands of years ago by the retreating Fox Glacier, which once reached to the sea's edge. A walk takes visitors around the lake edge to view one of the most photographed scenes in the country.

OPPOSITE: The alpine resort of Queenstown, also the country's premier adventure and adrenalin activity capital, sits on the edge of Lake Wakatipu with the Remarkables Range as a backdrop.

ABOVE LEFT: The coal-fired twin-screw steamer *Earnslaw* has plied the waters of Lake Wakatipu since 1912. The steel-hulled vessel made a daily commuter run between Kingston and Queenstown until 1969, after which it was restored for tourist cruises.

LEFT: The Catlins area, stretching from Waipapa Point in Southland to Nugget Point in South Otago, is noted for its coastal wildlife as well as beautiful valleys with gently flowing streams, such as the one descending gracefully through beech forest at Purakaunui Falls.

ABOVE: The Church of the Good Shepherd on the shores of Lake Tekapo, with the snow-capped Two Thumb Range beyond it, has one of the most picturesque alpine settings in the country. The 1935 building is a popular stop on the tourist trail.

OPPOSITE: New Zealand's highest mountain, Aoraki/Mt Cook rises 3754 metres beyond the head of Lake Pukaki. The glacier-fed lake is thick with suspended 'glacial flour', finely ground rock debris created by moving ice, which gives the water a distinctive pale blue colour. The summit of Mt Cook was first reached on Christmas Day 1894 by three New Zealanders. Hundreds have climbed the mountain since, but the ascent remains a considerable challenge.

OPPOSITE: Dunedin sits at the head of Otago Harbour, sheltered from the Pacific Ocean by the Otago Peninsula (*left*). At the tip of the peninsula on Taiaroa Head is a well-known colony of royal albatrosses. Other wildlife around the rocky coast includes penguins, albatrosses, seals and sea lions. The southern shore of the peninsula has quiet inlets and beaches, such as Smaills Beach (*right*).

LEFT: The ornate Dunedin Railway Station was built in Flemish Renaissance style.

ABOVE: Dunedin has many stately public buildings and private homes, fine examples of Victorian and Edwardian architecture.

NEXT PAGE: In Fiordland, Milford Sound winds inland for 22 kilometres from the Tasman Sea. The head of the sound is dominated by the majestic 1695-metre Mitre Peak.